Keri Glastonbury | Newcastle Sonnets

New Poems

GIRAMONDO POETS

Keri Glastonbury | Newcastle Sonnets

First published 2018
from the Writing & Society Research Centre
at Western Sydney University
by the Giramondo Publishing Company
PO Box 752 Artarmon NSW 1570 Australia
www.giramondopublishing.com

Designed by Harry Williamson
Typeset by Andrew Davies
in 10/16.5 pt Baskerville

Printed and bound by Ligare
Distributed in Australia by NewSouth Books

Cataloguing-in-Publication data is
available from the National Library of Australia

ISBN 978-1-925336-89-4 (pbk)

I think I was thinking
when I was ahead I'd be somewhere like Perry street
erudite dazzling slim and badly-loved

TED BERRIGAN 'PERSONAL POEM #9'

Contents

In Newcastle, in Tokyo...

Who knew when I read those sonnets
in the library, that I'd later be penning them
from an office in a world-class
'gumtree' university?
While you, the anti-Don Draper
of Shimbashi, can't even enjoy
a blade of grass
without a Suntory handy.
                    Oh public transport envy!
But here the beaches
are overexposed
        & underdeveloped,
the surfers are analogue & I still call the pelicans
at the Cowrie Hole, Mr Percival.

Hectic times at The Staysh
with its neon on the blink vs the Hoshino resort's
edamame on high. There's a Misao Okawa
in us all, drinking paleo hot chocolates
the way our ancestors made them.
Now, I'm hardly living in Detroit, though a local shop
sells pannikins & Mason jars, the post-industrial
as an *in situ* conceit. I may never build a hay bale shed
at Stroud, but there are small advances:
like how I can walk into a hospital ward without fainting,
read historical fiction, sleep in the same bed as someone.
I finished *Burial Rites* yesterday & finally switched
the car radio to ABC Classic FM,
surprised by the breakfast announcer's ums.

Goodbye to All That

Driving over Styx Creek, appropriately
laden with heavy metal.
The TAFE maintaining a cold shoulder,
where transgender trainee librarians from Kurri,
        meet Penny Wong's ex-speech writer,
                meet all the dropkicks.
Like watching *Orange is the New Black* thinking
there but for the grace of god… (& now whenever
I speak it's in Pennsatucky's accent).
The city's lazily retooled past lives,
a slurry of toxic carcinogens leaching from the gasworks
hidden in full public view.
Outside, parents are waddling their kids to school
—it could be the East Village.

Seeking neither the uniform distancelessness
of the network nor the uniform nearness of suburbia.
The perfect setting for an 'eat dirtzian' doctorate
as the longest goods train in the history
of Christendom passes the level crossing
—clanging like there's no tomorrow.
Hydraulic bottle jack signage snares
my ambient attention, on days when my interior
monologue is a triumphant coda
& I've cracked this city, such as it is.

Chasing muskrats down stormwater drains,
street wangs like modern fertility symbols
& mould swatches greening cement banks
tagged with Aspire & Prismo.

Minor aesthetic categories include
the interesting (in Martin's terms anything less
than marvellous). The felt inside a glasses case
means nothing to me, not even if I feel it,
passed around class like imitation birdcalls.
Across the street the baby boomer hippies
listen to the happy sounds of Africa,
or so they tell themselves until parole & PTSD.
Art school graduates working at Steggles chickens.
The night the car rolled & Reckless was blaring
like diegetic sound: we're all watching the same quality TV now.
Mojo may have long left town but there's still
a few *Los Chucos Suaves* hiding in the native grasses,
the world inside Clyde Street.

What Would I Say?

Dispersing a lyric via leaf blower
& other 80s cult songs like '88 Lines About 44 Women'
—what if John Forbes had lived
to live tweet during Q&A?
It's all lost generation stuff & the malls
were unindicted co-consipirators. Who knew?
Meaghan Morris/Maitland.
Joanie loves Chachi vs Date Academics in AU.
Blended learning sounds more like margarine,
getting a contact high off Islington
as cars widen through my fingers & toes.
We can have our little big smoke.
That BLF t-shirt was about to publish a poem.
It's the classiest butter chicken on earth.

Siobhan there's a keynote tomorrow
'*Mother I'm Rooted* to *Motherlode*'
sounds sexier than it is.
My hygienic lily is instant permaculture,
washed like a dirty golf ball.
Tess of the Erskinevilles played by young
beestung-lipped English actors.
Ah I saw that Mahavishnu Orchestra
cassette too, loaded up in my head the internet
is really flat & mirrors.
Spraying Aerogard *inside* my office!
Not so fond of formalities, like seeing the Vice Chancellor
in a waffle weave thermal.
I might be Adam Cullen & a degree of God.

Yeah I'd vote Tony Windsor
on a *Mad Men* mainline
with a Knitting Nancy from the farmer's markets.
No humanitarian relief, too many
French schoolboys *(petit ecolier)* & the ubiquitous
end of semester cold sore.
The thick oatmeal
of Sandilands' face   *ff'd up* bunny
a 2000-year-old twink.
A history of gay bars
jutting up against biker bars
in the middle of the genre.
Editor of repressed alignment issues
—Wallsend to Linda Ronstadt: 'You're No Good'.

Genius Loci

I never see Jane & Zorro
in the river gums, only Super 8 footage
of the ocean pool
at Fairy Bower, my mother swimming
laps along her perfectly ruled graph paper
—the cold affect of archival water.

Meanwhile, when it rains
Civic Station's trying
to be a Venetian canal
or urban dairy. Imagine ice-skating
the length of the CBD inside a Dune worm
—a New Babylon refracted in puddles.

Hallow the yellow brick
of the Carrington Pumphouse!

Olivia Rode Goodooga

Your brother's trick horses
going to seed like superannuated
rugby players, a tiny reliquary of Italian
bitumen wedged into your thigh
(the spirituality of sport).
These days you can catch a straightedge punk
food-blogging his morning eggs benedict
or a coal ship called 'Fiction'
loaded with speculative realism.

I've got Sam Wagan Watson's
Love Poems and Death Threats
by my bed tonight & I can't believe
you didn't stick around
for the ceiling fan.

Skye Is a 2 Bit Whore

The Nomads Motorcycling Club
are inviting local residents...   jumping castles
on Chinchen Street filled with April fools.
Walking down the drain
as a form of object-oriented ontology,
eventually finding every piece
of a child's rubber jigsaw mat
as the local kids obliviously
        trick or treat their HQ.

When I need to flatter it
I reference South King Street 20 years ago.
The pebblecrete poles of the East End
speaking to an historicist melancholy
plastered all over Instagram.

The soundtrack is still Bob Hudson
in the 70s,   'eh geday'
or mythic 80s youth working
at The Waratah Philadelphia Cream Cheese Factory
listening to 'How Soon Is Now?'.
We drive past the man in the doorway
like a Mayfield mood ring
taking the temperature of our fingers.
The Bowraville suspect pulls up to a roundabout
in Cardiff & somewhere a HiLux
dual-cab is flecked with Macedonian blood.

We're the girls least likely, poets
pissing down our own legs.

Delete all Newcastle stories!

Not saying I haven't been
on a good wicket, but I hardly qualify
as a colourful racing identity.
Old school pastoral care
meets tomorrow's sheep today!
A bit like advertising for a teenage dish pig
or complaining about noisy brakes on garbage trucks.
It takes a while to realise that the memory
is the system itself,
made up of millisecond mosaics
—sea slugs registering
        every pinch to the gill.

The newspaper tells me that, in America,
nine baby girls called Pistol were born last year.

Calliope Sits

While Shok busks
on Maitland Road
—you feel better
knowing he's out there,
doing it for all of us,
unlike Donald Trump
monstering Jennifer Hawkins.
Leo Malley shakes a fist
like earthquake damage to an awning
& outside the gallery, Brett Whiteley
has laid a *mothra* of an egg.
The aesthetic is a form
of white primitivism.
('I need big pan!')

Coal & Cedar

There's a middle-aged woman painting abstract
expressionism in Maryville & a valley full of
Rothko in the fluoro vest economy.
Reminds me of my OCD Downs brother's unnecessary
wardrobe (a cosplay council worker).
Driving past the Diocese, there's the besser block bingo hall
& the tribunal tucked around the corner (annulling).
There's always a local Weegee with his point & click:
the actual being virtualised & the virtual actualised.
I'm too lazy with a camera but I sometimes notice
a detail that proves I'm not a replicant,
like the milk bottle glass in the deco Dairy Farmers
building (now selling cars). As the white whale Migaloo
(with hardly a barnacle on him) sneaks past.

To Be Seen From Space

Throwing down the gauntlet with fairy lights & flowers
& a dozen *nasu dengaku* for the BBQ (rockets
blasting from the oval). She cut off
most of her friends over the last 12 months
& wonders why they now have no interest in her
        (& are filling my freezer with lasagna).

I would have fallen completely if it wasn't
for a few key mates
                & the residual toughness
of boarding school. A bloke dressed in a cow suit
another as a bicycle pump (the Kraftwerk 12"
sounds like gay porn if you close your eyes).

I have worked out there is a direct link to the quality of my day
& a morning run. Merewether was lousy with dolphin.

Gaslighting

Took me back to the Regent Street dinner party
that will live in infamy, starring Ingrid Bergman & her tagine.
Galling to see their sponsorship pages
for the Black Dog Institute. Did you know Tony Abbott
rode into Dubbo with the bunch?
Hate to sound like some kind of neo-con, but modern
psychology has gone a bit too far in the self-actualisation direction.

I was the saddest girl in Ubud
(great title for an autobiography of a Balinese goth).
Faux sheepish about her drunken spew—'My idea involves camels,
fireworks & plausible deniability'.

I, too, was looking at the Disneyland photograph thinking,
oh, right, OK, phew, she can't bust this family up
—they are *uber*!

Sonetto Alla Sua Donna

So, you've finally met your phallic mother
except she's rotting at the fangs—poor possum.
All those scarlet women!
Your P.E. teacher with big boobs
& false piety, the parish priest & her fur babies
blessing a donkey at Rutherford Telarah pet mass.
Now you're holed up in 'Cycling Camelot'
with a legendary flat screen.
'It's a whole new way of living'
was a prescient slogan, the plucky *domestique*
& her liabilities ride again (and again,
every Saturday). Stayed up late
to see you live from a milk crate
on the *Avenue des Champs-Élysées.*

Exit Note to Academia

The parallels are striking: the desacralisation,
shitting in their own nests, falling victim to hard arses
on the departmental Kool Aid. The question now
is how to come back from *persona non grata*?
At trivia at The G I learned that pulchritudinous
means beautiful, that I can't spell camouflage & that otitis
is an ear infection. I'm still haunted by David McDiarmid's
'I want a future that lives up to my past', but otherwise
rainbow aphorisms aren't my forte.
The beaches have been closed for 7 days, though ol' chompy
hasn't stopped Justin Norris surfing with his grommets
—Australian ecopoetics at its finest.
Newcastle Council suddenly the go-to guys for oceanography.

'The sea was angry that day, my friends.'

Hardly on Throsby

Fracking fluid has entered the groundwater at Gloucester
as shipyourenemiesglitter.com goes viral—the herpes
of the craft world. I'm out on my daily Cliff Young shuffle,
past the water dragon near the pallet storage, mud crabs
in the mangroves & fiery Robyn Gordons.
They say crows have exceptional facial recognition, hold
grudges, guarding the Carrington Bridge over troubled waters
more like murderous therapists, than captains of industry.
Hashtags call specific & heterogeneous publics into being,
built around ad hoc vernacular & memetic modes of expression
on this, the International Day of 'kiss a ginger'.
My morning begins with oil pulling, followed by ½ a sertraline
washed down with a macadamia milk, blueberry & cacao smoothie.

Long live stand-up paddle-boarders in biohazard suits.

How's the Serenity?

Wombats appear like body weather rocks,
forces of *shakti* gathering at dusk.
I want to walk among them in Rick Owens sneakers
& my Sea Shepherd t-shirt.
Bamarang's up the river, just the kind of place
Novocastrian yogis like to retreat with their neti pots,
dripping salty fluid out a nostril.
Those months of triangulation, lumps like poached pears
on porridge, hidden in tissue.
I haven't felt excluded from a clique for years,
but middle-aged women can obviously be just as matey
as the Berlin polyamory scene.
She's hitting him with a steel brush from Bunnings,
coldness & cruelty in Australian national parks.

The Production Hub

Thesis, anti-thesis & synthesis is the algorithm
running our lives, triadic arrangements
stuck on Canadian chairlifts.
Trust the Fiat dealer in Wickham to like utes & sob
when I go to get the keys
—welcome to struggle town (rinse & repeat).

The railway line gets dug up & artist impressions
emulate dreams of Copenhagen.
It can't be sanitary, Newy dogs
have the strongest immune systems
as tiny sourdough pizzerias spring up
jilting topographies.
                                        This summer

Sam Stosur better not choke!

D-I-V-O-R-C-E

Dear Tammy, I've landed in a Mary Gaitskill
short story full of hurting words
as paralegals teeter about
                    in zebra-striped pumps.
It's spatially televisual, spanning
all possible narrative strife
—a retro static pervading the Wallsend air.

All those nights
you spent sleeping in the back room
—just another high school teacher breaking bad!
I refuse to be a wounded antelope
& I see her as something of a hyena (though who's
scripting this shit, Ricky Gervais,
as it's simply not that funny).

A freak wave spews thousands of litres
of seawater over the breakwater
& a woman gets slammed onto the rocks,
walking past that sign we all mock
—the sheer pedestrian scale of a city
that still has a cathedral as its highest point.

Neither fluoride nor Phenergan will
enhance this performance.
Tell us again how you were a grouse beater
(said as if she should have known
—with all the propriety of a Type A
after one too many school fetes).

I'm watching a time-lapse video of Newcastle harbour
like it's a symphony of the city.

The Gun Club

Fiftieth birthday themes
pile up like mutton dressed as lamb,
make mine butterflied
        on the baby Q.
I'm still mouthing the words
while I dance,
pouting like Owen Wilson
        in my Oakleys,
every shot an album cover.

The best dress-up party
I went to was as sex tourists,
now 80s music is blaring over Fort Scratchley
& Hawaiian shirts
are newly sincere.

I used to get my hair cut
at Lunatic Fringe
or in an apartment in Gotham,
but scrambling for credentials
in the boondocks
is futile.   I was always dancing
on the inside, that's how music gets in
(through the ears, lapses into
a deep ecology
        like a no-dig garden).

Some people build theirs
with literature
        & poetry,
watching the coal ships kedge by.

Unilaterally Headfucky

I would have eaten out
at endless *nouveau cuisine* restaurants,
with foams & ox tongues.
Just slap me now & press those *doof doof*
headphones further in to your perilous eardrums
as you ride off on your active transport,
Brooks seat nestled in your snatch.

I need to learn how to wrangle flesh again.
I'm sorry I starfished.
It's a bit like working out
how people might navigate a city,
a weekend of gorilla paving
        & a dysfunctional council, as you fold
your voting slip into an origami crane.

Like that friend
who worked for Glencore said
'If you lay down with dogs
        you can't expect not to get fleas'.
What will it take to snuff me out?
What will it take to mobilise me?
Recycled wood panelling, exposed brick?
Appreciating the discord for its deviation
from an aesthetic expectation, or laughing
at the malaprop, not because I'm judgy or a snob.

Finally went in to The Lucky
the other day & was impressed
with the bathroom sinks

—even McCloy can do hipster better than me.

Just Quietly Babe

Dear Hamish, hello. It is 5.15 am.
Guess we're more West Coast
though our purloined letters
remind me of one of those Japanese novels
that we're serialising (active 5 m ago).
You're secretly 'emo'
underneath the footy jock
facade, as you start to warm
to the circumstances
that have been thrust upon you
& I dream
of a stomach scar
        trailing down
                to a strap-on.

You're totally rat-packy,
she's totally mind-gamey,
the poor school 'mom'
        doesn't stand a chance.
Went to one of those
new bars
        the other night
in the city,
it was
a diabolical disappointment
(so much salt
        on the lamb
I thought I'd die
                of a cardiac arrest)

& the owner
had a kind of deep
Bob Carr voice
that echoed
like a parochial spirit
undoing all the top knots
on the waiters.
Why won't my drugs
        work in this town?
Guess I'm kind of used
to it now,
the chicanery,
the chiaroscuro
        of coal dust & sand.

Manic Pixie Dream Girl

All these women want to live off grid,
keep bees, while Dad's mountain biking
in the Snowy Mountains,
past pyramids of brumby poo.
Always thought I'd return in the requisite Subaru,
looking 'feminine, marvellous & tough'.
I was ready to sign up for a retirement plan
when I saw her Facebook photos of various alps.
Gentle non-binary who will paint your likeness
in landscapes & teach you to read clues left by lichens.
Double denim in the dark. I'm the flat-chested one
& you can get out those puppies!

If only we could run away to New Mexico
—perhaps Agnes Martin was really our grandmother.

Everybody Loves (Raymond Terrace)

He's having a quiet dark stout
overlooking the bush on the back verandah,
—louche, like Bowie gracing a *Labyrinth* mural
on a Hunter Street shopfront hoarding.

I wanted to get my salad fingers into her, except
I was left feeling like Rainbow Dash
vomiting up prana!   Her tits floating free
in the pool, a white fedora,
some kind of flashback to the 90s.

It all boils down to having the right surface depth
fold upon fold as I wait patiently
for that James Turrell moment,
where I realise that we've been sitting in the dark
staring at a hole in the wall, productively.

A one-night stand
is just a video clip: like that friend
who still dines out
on being an extra in Adam Ant.
        But the Foreshore is no Le Mans,
        the only Monte Carlo are biscuits,
        driving past teenagers proudly sitting
        on the boot of a Barina.

There are still flashers at bus stops
but now the grapevine is virtual
& kids have *Fjällräven Kånken* backpacks
in candy colours.

The unbearable lightness
                                        of rail.

Cards Against Humanity

What is Batman's guilty pleasure?
Clive Palmer's soft, shitty, body.
Driving home from Mayf. Woolies turn right
at The Book Room (with its styrofoam boxes of weeds).
Months ago I was at your clinic for diazepam,
now I'm trying mindfulness to mollify
my inner-teen into some kind of luxe normcore.
A friend has fifty free-range guinea pigs
roaming her backyard on Sunderland St,
each one with an 80s haircut or innovative cowlick.
I was feeling oh so jaded until I watched Valerie Taylor
befriend a spotted moray eel off the Banda Islands.
Like her, I too, mistake
        muscle memory for affection.

Stay Gold Ponyboy

Some of the old fella surfers
have eyes as blue as the ocean, but you know it's bogus,
like un-signposted speak-easy bars.
The public secret is still knowing what *not* to know.
I don't vaccinate my kids (don't worry,
I don't have any).   Why not manifest
an ahistorical Chinatown
in the laneways or Spanish Steps up The Hill?
Every time I drive down Hunter Street I notice
that 'Asian Girls' sign on the turret & cringe.
If it was a real French Concession
we'd rope in some of Jean Genet's sailors.

I hear sometimes clients pay just to have
the blackheads on their backs burst.

Let’s go out, drink some locally fermented
Tumbarumba chardonnay, eat bagels
with pulled pork & apple slaw.
We never seem to stop coming of age,
our voices warbling like Jim Carroll
harking back to those sporting years.
Hillsong pastors are family planning
like it’s an all ages *bildungsroman*
                    with three stages of RAWK!
I lost my phone & realised how few
stakeholders there are left in my life.

She says her half-marathon days
are behind her as you both pose in tuxedos,
only one tie your own.

East Coast Low

Took ages to check
if you took the hiking tent, a work-around
for the hypervigilance of built-ins
Honey Badger is nasty!
As a neon Red Rooster sign is blown
onto Main St, Edgeworth, failing
to cross the road.

I've spent the last few days
showering in strangers' bathrooms
on Boatman's Row, dripping
on heated polished concrete.
A squatter in my own home like someone
who can't pay the utility bills
—Withnail covered in liniment.

It was tranquil by tea-light,
though I look nothing like my profile photo
of Myuran Sukumaran's self-portrait
nor Joyful Hours (a girl paddling
a red canoe).
I've fucked someone now
whose calves are even
thicker protrusions.
I hung out with Stella in Islington Park
yesterday & all the kids
were climbing over the felled gums.
Perhaps there is always a silver lining
—eating toasted granola at Dark Horse Espresso,
                    totally off the radar.

Life-changing Breakfast

Their propaganda is persuasive, but only some
beauticians believe it. Beaumont Street as a high street
heterotopia now serving 'upcycled' Greek heirloom yoghurt,
though adding adjectives won't stop the whiff
of pepper steak. She's looking $1M in her crop top
while you're still wearing Sportscraft no doubt,
a whole wardrobe abducted.

She's in a slinky tank as she crocodile smiles
& I hope you're full of chocolate bullets on Anzac Day.
The Californian bungalows signal an aspirational fault line,
the old steel lettering of the velodrome sign
a Euro style you purported to uphold.
I'm convinced by the apothecary nature of food, but this
sounds more like selling eggs on Christian values.

City of *Moi-Meme*

Chopping wood, carrying water gives my life
a certain backwoodsy zen, broken by a giant teddy bear
floating in Throsby Creek wearing some kind
of bespoke Speedos like Playschool (True Crime).
The post office caught in a perfect storm
of sovereignty—the anti-QVB!
Though who will man the phones of an NBN telethon?
Who goes to Pokolbin Pride?
The penis tower smells of urine,
as superphosphate wafts across the harbour.
I have studs in my ears made of local coal,
en plein air service stations hanging on the walls.

From below the bridge the neon reflections could be koi,
everyday rewards glimmering in karmic glissando.

Two Dog Night

On a trivia team
        with the sweetly diminutive
cross-dressers from Karuah.
Wanda looking Xanadu
in her diamante 'W'
(praising her wife's skill on a ride-on mower
while Kit's mansplaining in a pink lacy bra
                    —choofing on an e-cigarette).
I just want to join the boots over jeans club
but the retail experience
at the Rock Shop
        leaves a lot to be desired.

You're affecting my regional
identity on a cellular level.

Next, I'll write an experimental biography
of Renae Lawrence, starting with the day
her Staffy bit your hand at Horseshoe beach.
There's trauma at the heart
                                        of the recent past
& it's given me telepathy (when really I should
be signing a submission to the senate).
I won't survive around the fire pit,
splayed out like Mackie,
a barrel-chested Gentle Ben on tramadol
—a drug that helps my buddy in Darwin
with his yoga stretches.

The Islington figs release the bats & the sky
blacks out like an erasure poem.

Chronotope Hwy

The forgotten allure of conversations
inside cars, like fast & furious, but cooler.
We drop your brown dog in his many Pantone
shades at Cooranbong & kill get directions
—her indefatigable English accent permanently miffed
at being called to account for anywhere.

At the petrol station I feel like River Phoenix
as I'm always sleepy, though as soon
as we hit town you crave background noise.
You've got the pinball hips,
                                        as the multi-balls rain down,
though ordering fish this far inland is a risk.

Soon we're holed up in our executive apartment
by the mighty Murrumbidgee.

Two women enter…
Even Mum's sure she's met this one before,
like that *Seinfeld* episode when Elaine
decides to stay with her 'bizarro' friends.
On the back balcony, with a rubber tyre ashtray,
ugg boots & Sapporo the cockatoos are ecstatic.

Or we're having a Sunday roast chicken
expertly stuffed up the jacksie
until the drive home
spools on like archival footage,
passed the cli-fi wind farms
& a burger in Gunning.

Further north the Mooney Mooney windsock
deflates in pre-emptive despair.

Panic Attack in Maryville

My beautician isn't saving for a house deposit
in Elermore Vale, her husband's developing property
with a five-star green rating. I like the idea of being
part of a lesbian power couple & going into biz,
                                        …but big fish, small ponds.
Thank god we never got a foster kid & enrolled it
at The Junction, where 'manners maketh man'.

In the park Les gives her three boys 1/2 a prune each.
Steiner says every one of the four temperaments
will ideally grow into a more balanced adult.
I'm phlegmatic with a penchant for the sanguine,
while the choleric are having a Malcolm Turnbull moment.
Melancholics are poetic slaves to ideology,
                    wanting to get into that *Best Australian*.

Nobody Cares About Your Cat!

Bridget's being titty fucked in a Union Street strip joint,
as new dramaturgical questions are raised about bodies in space,
almost twenty years too late for Club Bent.
Location services switched off, like Facebook Freaky Friday.
P & P yet to make a cameo, waving from the powerboat.
At the vet I want to take a three-legged greyhound home,
fetishising her fine wire muzzle—though I'm not sure
I quite have the physique. Or is that coming from a narcissistic
place, like changing rescue pet names? In the film version
Bill Murray plays Hamish, Patricia Clarkson plays me
& I'd always cast you as Nic Cage in *Leaving Las Vegas*
as we shuck back oysters on my stoop.

I'm haunted by that woman we saw smoking in her Kingswood
& on a powerline in Lambton, a cockatoo screeches 'John'.

Why I Am Not a Painter

Locally grown persimmons
sit underneath a vase of wildflowers,
while your blind mini-Pincer
eats a Cadbury Picnic, his eyes a milky marble.
On the plane over I watched Amy Winehouse
get maggoted & then took Amy the duck
to the vet. She quacked as we sat in the waiting room
voicing something so guttural,
then shat all over the floor.

At the *yakuza onsen* I show my tattoos
& your back is covered in *yuzu* stigmata.
I'm an epic fail as a housewife,
getting older is a process of revising myself down
to some kind of Lissajous curve.

The signal-to-noise ratio,
a form of fine tuning
that continues over social media.
We take the definitive shot
on a bridge under the *momiji* & later
colour in Christmas cards for LGBTIQ prisoners
in America, as if singing 4 Non Blondes
is a real lifehack for global sensitivities
on gaycation.

It's feminist trivia night
at The Croatian Club
& my newsfeed finally tells me
Oscar Pistorius is guilty as fuck.

I guess that's why I'm a teetotaller.

D&M Kotara

You buy Rob Lowe's biography
out of a sales bin & tell me how actors
masticate to create empathy
(has the opposite effect on me).
An a-ha moment: that ex-junkie rat
raided your dog's painkillers,
perhaps she's high at a wedding
in Mildura as we speak.
They're on the rooftop getting
their Margaritas on, more retail whorehouses
sold by the square-metreage,
reclaimed timber to imbue meaning.

Or going to the brow bar
& coming out looking like Fozzie Bear.

Teralba Is Burning

I'm remembering a photograph
out the front of a fugu restaurant & a guy singing karaoke
in an empty laundromat, his warbling carrying out
onto the streets of Asakusa, through the gentle rain.
Takashi Murakami has painted 500 Arhats,
a post-tsunami superflat pilgrimage.
Now we know what happens after the 90s,
how we age thus far. There's even a Gen Y
fighter for arts funding who hails from Budgewoi.
I post a replica shot, armed with a *South Park* quote,
an iPhone & the Kübler-Ross model of grief.
Does anyone remember Alessi? His golden roof turdy thing?
Now I'm climaxing via Viber in Islington Park,
listening to your vocal fry.

An Evening with David Sedaris

The pirate & the skinhead of Chinchen Street
—head-kicking scurvy dogs.
Monty puts *Momochichi* into the cockpit
& bursts through the shopfront in a mankini.
Later, at the Civic, in-the-know Novocastrians
are lapping it up & I'm listening to people laugh
feeling disappointment at your empty chair.
The bunch riders are having a pool party
at Nesca Parade, something so American sit-commy
as she leaves her scent on the Crescent photo.
Peaches & the chick from Sleater-Kinney
are in this episode, as self-referential queer comedy
ends in an Indigo Girls sing-a-long.
No pink shirt will ever be enough.

All the Rivers Run

Murray Cod on the menu at Three Blue Ducks!
It was a good fight, with old mate back where he belongs.
You were squealing by a willow then spewing in *Star Wars*
(Carrie Fisher's coke habit started on set in episode 2).
If only our future interior was more like Julie Paterson's
blueprint for a life, we'd be twice lucky.

A mob in their knock-out guernseys set up on the bank.
Second holiday novel finished, too classical for my tastes
but I love the Nan Goldin shot on the cover.
The corroboree frogs in the Tumut information centre
are precious illuminations nestled in moss.
You're expectorating gunk in the shower, as the boot camp girls
thwack the pads like porridge popping on the stove.

The purple spinner, the scotch thistle.

The Scott Sisters

The Fernery stunk of mould
& Lynx before high tea & Ash Island
was once untrammeled. You're giving me
butterflies like a sketchy
natural history illustration MOOC
as I fill up a plastic bag
with duckweed.

Because we all know from the conception
of that thought to the reality of doing it
in the dyke world can be literal years.

Descendants of miners from Newcastle upon Tyne
gather around the Hexham mosquito
hoping for a meat tray win.

A telling bone chirps.

Cloudy with Chance of Rain

My Berlin girlfriend is at the dog park,
though really she went to Merewether High
as a giant pike eel washes up at Swansea & the *Herald*
takes a while to report whether it's been photoshopped
—a marine biologist providing expert opinion after noon.
Think of the *unagi don* thrashing around in a moonlit tinnie.
Or there's the vigilante approach, the Polaroids
of shoplifters in the tobacconist on Beaumont Street
busted for selling synthetic cannabis, a 'natural' herb
sprayed with chemicals. Prominent local police officers
& lawyers, dragging someone out of a party
as you recognise a local yokel putting cigars
down his pants. The *demimonde* is a slippery cusp
—the latest addiction sweeping Tomago steel.

The Sea Folding of Harri Jones

International city of cyclone fences, clearly the council
can't afford the upkeep. The Bogey Hole haunted
by a drowned Welsh poet, as skinny dippers slink
around from Suzie Gilmore at low tide.
Someone's doing *parkour* on the military ruins,
no one is washing up in Shepherds Hill cottage,
the ghost of artist-in-residence past. It's just more shit
academics say, nutscaping testicles at scenic vistas
meets birds with arms. In a parallel city
we sit at Redleaf pool & claim public space, trading in
any remaining identity politics. I've got enough history
to have been at Cafe Hernandez back in the day.
You're deciding whether to join Thai forest monks
in Western Australia, or the radical faeries.

Sloth or *pain au chocolat*?

Cushy lecturing job in a regional town,
working like it's still the 90s wardrobe-wise
as you appear in a midnight blue tuxedo—missed out
on Courtney Barnett at Bar On The Hill.
They say literature should be contested,
not agreed upon, though is getting square in a jerking circle
the gangland essay that destroys the Melbourne voice?
Has anyone done a PhD on defunct Australian theme parks?
The magic of Fantasy Glades, Port Macquarie.
Kissing fence posts like a Coogee Virgin
—*bork bork* giving a hecking sermon.
At a pirate party in King Edward Park, the kids line up
to pull strings out of the piñata (WTF!) while I've been
playing pin the tail on the donkey like it's a real animal.

This Is Newcastle

For all the history of the book it's come down to a selfie
of a middle-aged Brisbane poet crying in a mirror,
as ladyboys are heckled in Jesmond & Johnathan Thurston dons
rainbow laces. We take the elevator to level six of the new
courthouse & survey the view, wishing we were researching
a feminist legal thriller set in the Hunter activist community.
There's a pig's head on a spike on a fence
—it's Cooks Hill meets *Lord of the Flies*.
The magistrate's totally *cray cray*, you're downstairs
& I'm loitering by a roller door thinking of Nigel Milsom
living a quiet life with his muse.

On Sunday, we'll fish off a jetty at Bonnells Bay with mullet gut
as the lights come on at Eraring & somewhere, nearby,
there's a coal-fired hot spot for bream.

Easy Rider

Captain Pugwash arrives in Portly
on its maiden voyage
across the channel: the sea is rising,
                                        no more compromising.
Like Daniel Johns pulling up for durries
in his Jeep, the rewards of the graveyard shift
at the Merewether servo. Your modern lit lecturer's plaid shirt
collection rivalling that of a baby dyke.
Kristin Hersh at the Boree Creek Hall
with the deb ball decorations hung like huge tastebuds.
Home of my second cousins.
Newcastle? Might as well be *Cinque Terre*.
The drone above the dog beach captures the kayaks
like blood platelets, or e-coli.

The Star Hotel

The first Australian dictionary
& significant autobiography (a flashy memoir)
penned at Coal River, half of Dyke Point ballast
from Haight-Ashbury
(any Englishman's
chance to say Nobby's on the telly!).
If there's a riot, we'll be doing a Sharpie dance
—the gays, the merchant seamen, Stella the Fella.

The shame of a criminal record
saw him stop the grog & leave Mayfield
before he turned twenty. Now he's a harmless
trainspotter, passionate about rail trails
in the South West Slopes.

I'm the phoney with the 'All Stations' tin sign.

My Brilliant Friend

Today I got a haircut off a seminal member
of Bitchcraft, she offered to lend me her plastic
toboggan from Aldi if it's still in one piece.
She likes comedies (like my neighbour)
but I never laugh intentionally, or I feel manipulated.
It's why I read the spoilers, though sometimes
I make analogies before the recaps do,
our collective conversation like a drip filter talk poem.
The way we talk though, is still something special.
It belongs to the era of arcades, of an arcadia illuminated
in oil paint on Belgian linen, not to be confused with
Anthropologie sofas. Two artists from Maitland
have made it big in the metropolis, both
grew up, no doubt, on Neapolitan ice cream.

Friday Feels

A Watt St immunologist is up on 80 sexual assault
charges as a local artist tapestries You Filthy Bastard
onto a chux, FRIGHT & FLIGHT onto his pillows.
I'm so conflicted by this session's trend in undergraduate lingo
—personally, I feel… (Bernie Sanders is too idealistic).
Increasing exposure to other people's perspectives
producing empathy as a shield.

What is a normal commodity?
At what point on the pack or lock-out?
Like a mini-mental exam to spell world backward.
Is it *schadenfreude* to want Westconnex to deadlock
King Street, Newtown (not King St, Newcastle)?

In Monaco, there's a stunning Torres Strait Islander roof-top
mosaic—spinning our noses around to find our cringing faces.

High Swan Dive

The night before the election, the local member
attends the exhibition opening of a Lithuanian painter.
Up on the staircase, the architect trembles.
There's a politic to this town that I'm just getting
the gist of—my own legacy built at the coal face,
the omen as contested as a willy-wagtail sighting.
It's about funerals, whose? & the fear of a drubbing
at the ballot box. No way I want to retire to Pleasantville.
The young are already scoping out Sandgate
for that 1950s weatherboard dream, growing vegetables,
making beetroot brownies. Any further north & you'll get
One Nation outpolling the Greens at the St Brigid's
booth in Raymo. I'm chatting to a woman whose
cancer has returned, asking for second preferences.

Steve Price Says

The inquest into Stacey's murder starts tomorrow
—the dumb & dumber defence.
If you ever feel the need to score pink ice at 4 am
Dallas has directions to the zoo.
All I remember of Caves Beach is the fugly architecture,
now kids on surf skis infiltrate hidden chambers
with their go-pros. Public memorials line the Stockton side
of the breakwater, dating back to the 1980s:
plastic carnations & DIY rock art amongst a colony
of feral cats. It's locals only, but tell Sonia Kruger
that being a mother is not border patrol.
Not a Pokémon in sight! We're drinking gin
at The Maryville Tavern—pressed metal ceilings
designed by Brad & Lara from *The Block*.

The Priests

I'll confess to you, I never liked
the crying child Hit the Bricks mural
either. Figurative language is less
comprehensible & on that street corner it's been painted black.
There's two words, one finger as the local teenagers ink themselves
& demand a new romanticism of art. Death over Dinner is cancelled
at Wests sundered in the transition
from on-line to off. Out the back lane
behind Suspension a woman is living
with broken ribs from chemo.
Native flowers line her nature strip.
Her son, his softness (campy, but not
arch) serves up coffees with a goofy gait
—confidence in community standing.

Suburban Sakura

Arthur Wicks inspects spray cans left behind
by vandals, as hoons terrorise Willans Hill.
A lone shopping trolley carcass rusts at the rocks
& a rope swing hangs typographically.
From farm to table North Wagga style,
the neighbour's goat off limits on social media,
yelling like humans. Peppercorns smelling
of childhood, magpies swooping reflector
Lululemon horns, jogging past the
plum blossoms that line Pinnaroo Drive.
My brother posing in hibiscus Okanuis
& a Ramones t-shirt, memories
in the font of The Shanty Tavern.

Legal Aid Newcastle (no caller ID).

The Pink Flamingo (of Trespass)

Is anyone else getting memories that aren't theirs?
Photographs of other people's children?
A bush doof in the Watagans?
The Tromp family's psychedelic road trip
unfolds like a Netflix *folie à deux*
as Shakespeare's Sonnet 127 is read in Noongar.
I'm on a giant inflatable, while a spoonbill
fossicks in the billabong like something from Dr Seuss.
A sacred kingfisher outlines the parabola
of my crap bird photography.
Twitchers of the North Wagga mudflats!

    The fresh water gooseberries on my skin
are free of salt,   no turquoise bleachers
    against these sadcore skies.

Deconstructed Toast

The speed of spines makes my reading body
obsolete, more like a hospital ward visit:
obligatory, confronting, like cankles
& stove-top thighs.
Unlike you, I have no conception
of what meat weighs, a chronic lack of detail
about the chain of events that leads to the cashier.
The obsidian smear more offensive, yet more 'our town'
than the equivalent in lemon meringue.

Felching flowers in the hotel lobby,
flannelette shirt patchwork curtains in the Airbnb
like a form of bogan *borro*.
We're bringing pocket equality
                                        to women's pants.

Plastic Newcastle

Home renovation compensating for the lack
of trees & thumping ocean baths
deliver expanse. Curlicues of lime-burning
smoke, fuelled by middens filled with oyster shells
like shaking a Barrington Tops snow dome
& watching those Tasmanian Devils
chowing down on carrion comfort.
The King of Woy Woy not available
to quell this uprising & I'm not Catholic
or convict, statistically more artists than miners
—the synthetic intellectualism of a hard hat.
We return Bear the 3-Legged Wonder Dog
to Cafe Inu
    with a puncture.

Kill Your Sensor

A Little Life
—unfinished,
preferred *The Flamethrowers*.

Post-divorce, life is unanticipated,
adulting as a verb.

Post-internet, life
is never fully encapsulated
& yet writ large, toiling like

digital deckhands. Brexit
as a brand of laxative.

Be sure to take
the steering wheel
off lock
exiting the Cahill Expressway.

2 Hours South

Trudging behind a fresh crop of profile photos
wearing heavy boots, the lurker as liminar
—even rainy Sundays in Tinseltown
feel post-celebratory. I'm exactly where I want to be,
full of shakshuka. There's all sorts of margins
from Warrimoo
                                    to Wahroonga, as mutable
as the idea
of commutable distance.
We're making Sydney into a kind of op shop string art.
A farrago of ways to be jealous, ways to be vicarious
ways to suffer, swiped away like old screens.

Let's take Eileen Myles
to The Bearded Tit.

The White Bird

Life imitates art,
a finger-wagging biddy intercepts my darling
in a staged startle reflex. Cindy Sherman or
Caravaggio in Cessnock Correctional Centre?
A felted dream of floating green pool tables,
that graffiti in the women's cell:
'feed Mal Pal'.
The metropolitan critic comes to town
& goes only to the regional gallery
—a poetry of complaint, misses the authenticity
of the drying paint. The blacks,
the Prussian Blues.

His sister is on the radio, who knows left from right?
'even stinky ibis seem majestic'.

Sad Chairs of Academia

A study in inertia (the struggle is real)
suspiciously stained,
hard truths that can't even be
considered retro (Emmett's joke
                                        in the Maths building).
Unfolding in the fits & starts of on-line time.
Discussing the American election
over dinner: John Frow & I
both alumni of WWHS.
What if the Murray River was a person?
What if I don't love Dick?
If we're such a Goldilocks City, I'm having
more porridge.

Let's hope Danni Roche uses a stick to the shins.

Deep Water

Noah Taylor's catfish mo, was it him
or Ben Mendelsohn I saw at The Sports Bar?
Park Side Killers hardly shitting themselves cross-platform.
The same honeycomb cliffs, Hawkesbury River sandstone
from way before Sam de Brito's time.
Phone numbers scrawled on public toilets
as far north as Birdwood Park.
Pushed out of the corporate memory
cis-men watching SBS with their sons & daughters,
a checkered privilege beneath that down-at-heel leather jacket.
Cleveland Street High boys equating paedophiles & poofs.
It's E-Street meets *A Clockwork Orange*,
brandishing a giant white penis.
Even the scummy perpetrators now have profiles.

Penguin Bloom

My best friend Ploppy disappeared this morning
he's a cane toad of the sky, real ingénue of Lake Macquarie
where perception forgets itself without reflection.
Drifting through storage sheds, 'we are the cheapest'
the bragging rights of spectacular discourse,
'pure dance' on a wheelie bin.   See, he really is her best friend,
the opportunistic bullying of his species is not his fault
the Indian Myna & intersectionality.   We're all aiming
for I-don't-mindfulness, the poetic ideal of a Dreamworld
run by ardent leisure.   It's like asking a magpie
to spell that, pink-ifying pellets to create aesthetic
standards in farmed salmon. I'm glad I live in a world
where women with PCOS are growing lady beards
& Hillary uses her first name.

Rough & Tumblr

Disturbingly indicative of a blow-in, blow-hard generation
—the changing of the guard in a discipline meeting
little more than a cargo-cult radio of coconuts & straw.
The poets/songwriters of the 80s are now in churchy bands,
bespoke gold-leaf surfboards poking out of Sandmans.
Post-war, when wanting to be something other than a boiler-maker,
a nurse or an engineer, was to be a pariah.

Looking wistfully up towards Segenhoe (no longer precariat,
but never proletariat). I just met an ex-Castanet Club member
on a lesbian dating site, with ties to a group of MILFs
whom I've bracketed off as missed friendship opportunities.
Jenny Brockie's not really much of an empath,
like that screen-writer guy who up & moved to LA
when the vigilante squad outed him as Sylvia Plath.

Who Killed Bambi?

'I am in training, don't kiss me'
CLAUDE CAHUN

Her father coined a word—solastalgia,
a six-inch valley through the middle of Bulga
—she's an anthroposcenester, the full cast
of *Girls* in every class, like every town
has a Kurt Cobain. He likes to think the 'et pain' sign
on the pylon once said forget pain
—toughen up princess & take a spoonful of cement.

Crocheting iced vovos on the train
from the Sutherland Shire & coming up for TINA
her frilly white socks pre-puberty blues,
like Sylvanian families struggling to describe
a genre that we now know as reality.

I just had venison with Michael Leunig,
in a local hatted restaurant.

Re/form School

They had not read their Foucault in the 19th century,
adolescent scum of Sydney stitched up in James Fletcher,
for living with thieves or prostitutes.
If those ghost girls do form a band catch them
at The Lass. Oh Agnes King (aka 'The Freak')
we both arrived via Randwick & its bricks by the sea,
though nowadays 'Bankies' smoke on the rocks at the
women's pool recovering from Club Arak.
The girls riot—burning straw, ramming the doors of solitary.
The punishment is total Britney Spears
(low-diet & head-shaving). James Schuyler's
'back on antabuse', lead him not into Tempe Station!

My inner-inmate still wants to escape down
at the docks, but I wear a plain brown tunic.

Acknowledgements

Some of the poems in this collection (or earlier versions) have previously appeared in *A Slow Combusting Hymn*, *Cordite*, *Overland*, *Rabbit*, *TEXT*.

Many lines have been bricolaged from social media and personal correspondence, such as blogs, comment threads, SMS, Instagram handles, Facebook messages and newspaper headlines. My thanks to those with unacknowledged turns of phrase that I have appropriated and decontextualised as part of this recombinant poetics of place.

The Giramondo Publishing Company acknowledges the support of Western Sydney University in the implementation of its book publishing program.

This project has been assisted by the Australian Government through the Australia Council, its arts funding and advisory body.